THE GREAT BOOK OF ANIMAL KNOWLEDGE

FLAMINGOS

The Bright Pink Dancing Birds

All Rights Reserved. All written content in this book may NOT be reproduced in any form or by any means, including scanning, photocopying, or otherwise without prior written permission of the copyright holder. Copyright © 2014

Some Rights Reserved. All photographs contained in this book are under the Creative Commons license and can be copied and redistributed in any medium or format for any purpose, even commercially. However, you must give appropriate credit, provide a link to the license, and indicate if changes were made.

Introduction

Flamingos are big, pink birds found in huge groups. They wade in shallow waters looking for food most of the time. They also spend lots of time cleaning themselves and they even sometimes dance together! Let's learn more about this unique bird.

What Flamingos Look Like

Photo by Marcus Meissner(flickr.com/marcusmeissner), as licensed under CC BY 2.0 Generic

Flamingos are big birds with very, very long legs. They have a long, curved beak and a long slender neck. Their ankles are found high above the ground, some people mistake it for their knees. Their feet are webbed like the feet of a duck; it helps them balance while wading.

Size and Weight

The size and weight of flamingos differs between species. The biggest flamingo is the greater flamingo. They can grow almost 5 ft (1.5 m) tall! Flamingos are surprisingly light for their size. Greater flamingos only weigh up to 8.8 pounds (4 kg)! The smallest species of flamingo is the lesser flamingo. They only grow less than 3 ft (90 cm) and only weight around 5.9 pounds (2.7 kg).

Beak

The long, curved beak of flamingos is colored black on the tip. Flamingos have a unique beak that perfectly suits the way they eat. Flamingos feed by scooping up water and food on their beaks.

Neck

The long, slender neck of a flamingo is also important for the way they eat. Because their legs are very long, flamingos need long necks to reach down to eat their food. Their flexible neck also allows them to preen all parts of their body.

Legs

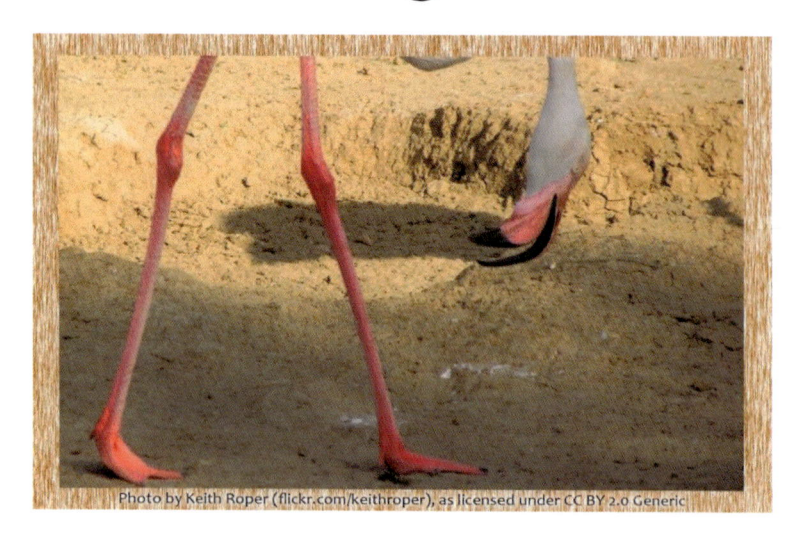

Photo by Keith Roper (flickr.com/keithroper), as licensed under CC BY 2.0 Generic

People used to believe that flamingos don't have knees. They actually have knees located high up on their legs and hidden under their feathers. The long legs of flamingos allow them to wade on deeper waters while looking for food. Flamingos can also run fast with their long legs to escape predators.

Flying

Despite their big size, flamingos are still able to fly because they are very light. They can fly up to 35 miles an hour (60 kmph). People don't usually see flamingos flying around. In fact, it was believed that flamingos don't fly at all! Flamingos fly during nighttime, this is why they are hardly seen flying. When food is scarce, flamingos have to fly for long distances to find new food sources.

Where Flamingos Live

Photo by Adam Baker (flickr.com/atbaker), as licensed under CC BY 2.0 Generic

Flamingos can be found in Africa, Asia, southern Europe, South American, Central America and the Caribbean. All flamingos need is a lot of food and a lot of water to survive. They prefer warm lowlands but they also live in colder environments such as mountainous areas.

What Flamingos Eat

Photo by Valdiney Pimenta (flickr.com/valdiney), as licensed under CC BY 2.0 Generic

All of a flamingo's food comes from the shallow waters that they wade in. Their main diet includes algae, crustaceans such as shrimp, mollusks, and small fishes.

Eating

Photo by James St. John (flickr.com/jsjgeology), as licensed under CC BY 2.0 Generic

Flamingos use their legs to shake up the water and mud and bring their food close to the surface. Once it's there they will then scoop up their food with their big beaks. Flamingos use their tongue and hairs in their mouth to filter out the water and mud from their food. All of this happens while the flamingo's head is upside-down.

Color

The color of flamingos varies from what type of food they eat. There are orange, red, and pink flamingos. Did you know that flamingos are not born pink? Flamingos are born with grey feathers. They turn pink, orange, or red because of the food that they eat.

Colonies

Flamingos are social animals and they can be found in big groups called colonies. There are sometimes more than a thousand flamingos in one colony! Flamingo colonies have many different dances and displays that all members join in. These include marching, head flagging, and wing saluting.

Grooming

Photo by Chad Sparkes (flickr.com/chad_sparkes), as licensed under CC BY 2.0 Generic

Flamingos spend a lot of time preening. They produce oil on the base of their tails and use their beaks to spread this oil on their feathers. Flamingos also like swimming to keep their feathers clean.

Sounds

Photo by Benjamin Radzun (flickr.com/2e14), as licensed under CC BY-SA 2.0 Generic

Flamingos cannot sing beautiful songs like some other birds. Instead they make squawking noises. The sounds they make are quite similar to the sounds of a duck.

Breeding

Flamingos don't have a yearly mating season. They usually mate after rains. The dances and displays of flamingo colonies are rituals that they perform to find a mate. Flamingos usually only lay one egg at a time because of its size.

Nests

After mating both parents have to build a nest for their egg. This is hard work and it can take quite a long time before it is built. Flamingo nests are made from different items such as mud, stones, twigs and feathers. When it's built, it looks like a mini volcano. Both parents take turns guarding the nest and incubating the egg.

Baby Flamingos

After about a month, the eggs finally hatch. Flamingos are born with grey feathers and a straight beak. Newborn flamingos drink crop milk. Crop milk is milk that is produced in the parent's digestive system. Parent flamingos will bring up the milk for their babies to drink.

Life of a Flamingo

After about a week, baby flamingos will leave the nest and join the colony. The adults in the colony teach the young how to swim and how to search for food. Flamingos reach maturity when they turn six years old. They usually live 20-30 years.

Sleeping

Flamingos have an unusual way of sleeping. When they sleep, they stand with one leg only! This is because only half of their body is asleep. The other half, the one with the standing leg, is still awake. After resting one side flamingos will then switch the standing leg and rest the other half of their body.

Predators

Flamingos have only a few natural predators. Birds of prey such as --- sometimes eat young flamingos and flamingo eggs. Big cats, wild dogs, and pythons also sometimes eat flamingos but they are not really their preferred prey. Flamingos are also hunted by humans for their meat. In some places, flamingo meat is a delicacy.

Species

There are six species of flamingos in the world. They all look similar and behave similarly, but there are some differences between them. Greater and lesser flamingos are found in Africa, Asia, and southern Europe while Chilean, Andean, James', and Andean flamingos are found in South America, Central America, and the Caribbean.

Get the next book in this series!

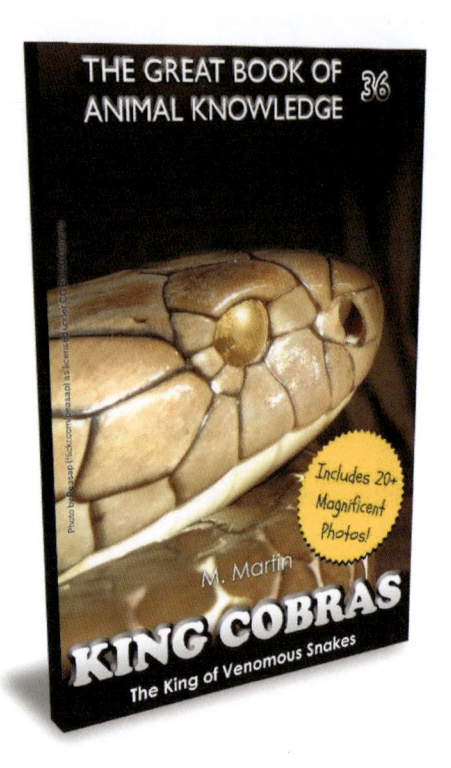

KING COBRAS: King of Venomous Snakes

Log on to Facebook.com/GazelleCB for more info

Tip: Use the key-phrase "The Great Book of Animal Knowledge" when searching for books in this series.

For more information about our books, discounts and updates, please Like us on FaceBook!

Facebook.com/GazelleCB

Printed in Great Britain
by Amazon